Welcome

This book should help you to make the most of your visit to York Minster. It was built to lift your spirit with devotion and delight and designed as a foretaste of heaven. Look up, because the Minster was designed to be full of light and space. The result is a series of huge and lovely spaces, changing with every hour of the day. Look around you, too: note the details of the carvings on every pillar and the proportions of the arches and windows. See how the ancient glass lets the sunlight through and changes it. You could visit this place every day for a lifetime and still be noticing new things.

This is a living place, built for daily worship. While you are visiting, there will probably be pauses for prayer. There may well be services in the chapels or in the quire. Please join us if you wish. Even outside the services themselves there are often events being rehearsed or taking place, because this is a place where things are always going on. Light a candle and say your own prayer.

Do not miss the Chapter House, one of the most beautiful rooms ever created. You can go down to the crypt and its treasures, or up to the top of the tower, with the best of all views of the city of York. Notice the inscriptions on the walls: they record kings and archbishops, nobles and ordinary citizens, as well as those who died in many wars. They belong to every generation since the building of the Minster.

Visit slowly. And often, in the years to come, think of us.

Keith Jones

The Very Reverend Keith Jones, Dean of York

Introduction

Y ork Minster is situated in the north of the walled city of York, formerly within a walled and gated enclave but now within a close of both parkland and historic buildings. The seat of the Archbishop of York, the Cathedral and Metropolitical Church of St Peter is the mother church of the Northern Province and the cathedral for the diocese of York, a centre for Christian life in the north of England.

To the east of the Minster lies the Minster School, a day school for children aged 3–11 where the boy and girl choristers of the Minster choirs are educated. Around to the north-east is St William's College, a magnificent timber-framed building dating from 1461 and formerly the home of the chantry priests who sang masses for the dead at altars in the Minster prior to the Reformation. Now used as the Minster's conference and banqueting centre, some of the medieval rooms are open to the public, as bookings permit. These include the exceptional 'Painted Chamber' with its surviving panels of original wall painting from the early sixteenth century. The college also houses the Centre for School Visits, our education service which works with tens of thousands of children each year, helping them to understand the beauty of the Minster and the lives, technologies and faith of those who created it and those who continue to work in it.

To the north of the Minster lies Dean's Park, created in the nineteenth century when buildings abutting the Minster were cleared away. The cobbled road into the park leads you past the Treasurer's House (now National Trust), formerly the home of the richest official of the Chapter in the Middle Ages; past the canons' houses and deanery; and on to the Minster Library and Archives. Open to the public for reading and research five days a week, the building incorporates the former chapel of the now-vanished medieval archbishop's palace, which occupied the whole of the north side of the Minster. Housing the Minster's archives and a working library of over 120,000 volumes, it is the largest cathedral library in the country. Alongside the library, the only other remnant of the palace is the fragment of arcading now incorporating the Kohima memorial.

Leaving the park at the west end of the Minster, you pass through the site of one of the former gates to the Minster's precinct and can look across to St Michael le Belfry church. Rebuilt by the Dean and Chapter in the 1530s, it was once the detached belfry of the Norman Minster and is now the parish church of the parish in which the Minster is housed.

The south side of the Minster faces down Stonegate into the city and the south transept has always been the entrance by which civic parties have entered and left the building. It is now the main entrance for visitors to the Minster, where we welcome you into 2,000 years of history and a vibrant Christian community.

Above View of the library, archives and Kohima memorial across Dean's Park

A testament in stone…

Right An eagle 'quarry' from the glazing of the Zouche Chapel, a chapel reserved for private prayer off the south quire aisle

The Minster site has been occupied for nearly 2,000 years, from the founding of the great Roman fortress of Eboracum in AD 71 to the glories of the building you see today. Little is known of the Christian community of Roman York; documentary evidence records a 'Bishop Eborius' attending the Council of Arles in AD 314, so there must have been Christians in this area prior to that, but it would seem that they largely disappeared in the years following the Roman withdrawal in the early fifth century. According to the writings of the Venerable Bede, Christianity returned to York in 625 when Paulinus, Saint and Bishop,

*Far left "God creates humankind
in His image" in the Genesis
order, Great West door, 1998
Left Shields of medieval donors
adorn the nave's soaring arches
Above View of the restored
Great West window and doorway
Right West front viewed from
Duncombe Place*

accompanied the Christian Princess Ethelburga
from Kent to Northumbria to marry King Edwin,
a pagan. Two years later, Paulinus baptized
Edwin and his court in a small wooden church
specially constructed for the occasion. This
building is always considered to have been the
first York Minster, although its exact location
is unknown. This building was in turn replaced
by a stone church, which was restored and
extended prior to its virtual destruction in 1069
during William the Conqueror's 'Harrying of
the North'. The Norman archbishop, Thomas
of Bayeux, built his great cathedral here
between 1080 and 1110; this was modified
and extended in the mid twelfth century by
Archbishop Roger de Pont L'Èvêque, who built
a magnificent new quire.

*A noble building, in view at least
30 mile before you come to it*

Diary of Celia Fiennes, 1685

*Overleaf Sunlight through
the stained glass fills the
south quire aisle with a
kaleidoscope of colours*

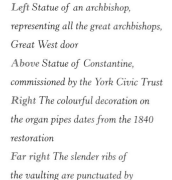

Left Statue of an archbishop,
representing all the great archbishops,
Great West door
Above Statue of Constantine,
commissioned by the York Civic Trust
Right The colourful decoration on
the organ pipes dates from the 1840
restoration
Far right The slender ribs of
the vaulting are punctuated by
elaborately carved bosses

Right A grotesque face-puller
supports an empty niche

The Undercroft contains the remains of some
of these earlier structures, but the present
building was begun in 1220. Archbishop Walter
Gray and the Dean and Chapter decided to
rebuild the Norman cathedral on a scale to
exceed Canterbury. The south transept was the
first section to be rebuilt; that and the structural
work of the north transept were completed by
about 1253. The next phase was the building
of the engineering marvel that is the Chapter
House; its great dome is spectacular in having
no central column to support it. Work began
on the nave in 1291, replacing the already large
Norman nave with what was to become the
largest medieval hall in England, completed in
the mid fourteenth century. The last major phase
of rebuilding included the quire and east end,

with the whole work taking over 250 years to complete. During the last phase, in 1407, the central tower partially collapsed and grandiose plans to surmount the tower with a belfry and spire were abandoned when cracks in the rebuilt stonework showed that the foundations could take no more weight. The building was considered complete enough in 1472 for a service of consecration, although the western towers were still unfinished.

The chantry altars and St William's Shrine – such prominent features of the medieval Minster – were swept away by the tide of the Reformation in the sixteenth century, and by the early nineteenth century the Minster's interior was a pale shadow of its former self. Two serious fires – in the quire in 1829 and in the nave in 1840 – destroyed the roofs of both areas and the woodwork of the quire, but the biggest threat to the Minster's survival was discovered in 1967. Widening cracks showed that the foundations were moving: a five-year rescue operation was launched, the results of which can be seen in the Undercroft. Another devastating fire in 1984 destroyed the roof of the south transept, but once again the skills of many, including the Minster's own workforce, restored the building's former beauty. Today we welcome a million people a year as visitors, worshippers, and pilgrims to admire this testament of faith.

South Transept

The south transept is the earliest part of the present building. Begun in 1220, it was largely the vision of Archbishop Walter Gray, whose Purbeck marble and limestone tomb you can see here with its effigy and elaborate canopy. His rounded, complex arches in the arcading above you are quite different from the pointed, simpler arches below and show how he was building at the point of transition from one style to another. Originally conceived as one of the great processional spaces, linking with the city along Stonegate to the river, the south transept is nowadays where visitors are welcomed and where they get their first taste of the size and beauty of the Minster. In the south wall is the famous Rose window, its stonework of 1240

Above View across the south transept into the north at triforium level showing the 'Benedicite' bosses
Right "O let Israel bless the Lord": Jewish head and Star of David boss carved by Geoff Butler

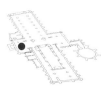

Above The famous Rose window was painstakingly restored after the 1984 fire by the York Glaziers' Trust
Right "Three men in a fiery furnace with protecting angel": boss carved by Fiona Bowley

containing the later sixteenth-century glass in the form of Tudor roses from which its modern name derives. Damaged in the fire of 1984, which destroyed the roof, the restored window was called the Marigold window for many years, reflecting the shape of the tracery, before the term Rose window was coined. The restored roof has 68 colourful bosses, depicting the words of the *Benedicite*, or the great ancient hymn of praise. These words sit alongside the six original bosses that could be saved from the fire and the six bosses designed by young winners of a competition organised by the children's television programme *Blue Peter*. They represent significant events of the twentieth century and include one of the fire itself.

We had to recreate a masterpiece

Bob Littlewood, Clerk of Works, on the restoration after the 1984 fire

Above Arcading detail showing Early English style
Left Dragon eating its own tail: a detail from Archbishop Walter Gray's tomb

11

South Quire Aisle

The south quire aisle leads you into the east end of the Minster and contains some of the finest polychrome memorials in the Minster, as well as giving you a glimpse into the eastern crypt below. On the south wall is hung the Great Processional Banner, depicting the crucifixion on one side and Christ giving St Peter the keys to heaven and hell on the other. Made in the 1920s, it is carried in procession at major cathedral services. Nearly opposite the banner on the north side are two cases containing the Minster's gilded processional cross and the delicate crystal primatial cross of the Archbishop of York. Set into the panelling, also on the north side, is the curious polished wood memorial to members of the Gale family. Made

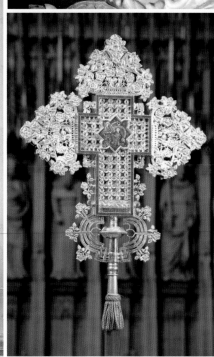

...by the aire and mien he looks more like a Soldier or a Beau than a Bishop, and so it seemes he was in humour

Diary of Celia Fiennes, 1685, on Archbishop Lamplugh's memorial

in 1963, it incorporates a jester's head and two coats of arms, which once formed the lid of a chest from the household of the Gale family. George Gale was Mayor of York in 1556 and his descendant, Thomas, was Dean of York in 1702. On the south side is the entrance to the Zouche Chapel, reserved for private prayer, and several highly coloured sixteenth and seventeenth-century memorials, including that of Archbishop Matthew Hutton and the perpetually angry-looking Nicholas Wanton. On the north side, next to the grilles into the eastern crypt, are the two great medieval cope chests, in which were once stored flat the heavily jewelled and embroidered cape-like robes of the clergy, worn when celebrating Mass.

Top Detail from the tomb of Archbishop Matthew Hutton, died 1606
Above Processional cross, 1912
Above right Christ gives the keys of heaven and hell to St Peter: detail from the Great Processional Banner

All Saints Chapel

Sanctuary lamp

This chapel at the east end of the north quire aisle was dedicated in 1923 and furnished to be the regimental chapel for the Duke of Wellington's Regiment. It contains a number of regimental items including framed 'colours', a roll of honour, and chairs with memorial brass nameplates. The richly embroidered dossal behind the altar depicts the crowns of all the saints ascending to heaven and was made by the Broderers' Guild in 1974 when the chapel was refurbished. Its rich colour complements the elaborate altar reredos with its gilded plaques of the four evangelists and the *Agnus Dei*. One of the most arresting sights, however, is the large monument of 1695 on the south wall to William Wentworth, 2nd Earl of Strafford, and his first wife by the sculptor,

John van Nost the Elder. The chapel is separated from the surrounding area to the west by wrought iron railings, made in 1930 to a design based on those in the fifteenth-century chapel of the Palazzo Pubblico in Siena, which continue around to the north side. Complementing the separation of this chapel from the adjacent Lady Chapel are the remains of the soaring canopied tomb of Archbishop Henry Bowet (died 1423). Badly damaged in the fire of 1829, which gutted the quire, the delicate vaulting of the canopy and the fine pinnacles were restored from scattered fragments by the craftsmen of the Minster stoneyard in 1981–3. This chapel is in regular use today for one of the daily celebrations of Holy Communion.

Top Detail from the tomb of Archbishop Tobie Matthew
Above Railing detail showing battle dates
Above right View into the chapel through the tomb canopy to Archbishop Bowet, died 1423

To see the early morning sun shining through …is to view the combined beauties of nature and art as they are rarely found

All Saints Chapel, Minster Guidebook, 1930

Lady Chapel

Originally filled with the tombs and memorials of cathedral dignitaries, and badly damaged in the 1829 fire, the Lady Chapel is part of the square-ended English-style fourteenth-century east end of the Minster and was restored for worship in 1883. Today it contains the monuments of several archbishops and one archbishop's wife – Frances Matthew, wife of Tobie Matthew. It was her gift to the Minster in 1627 of Archbishop Tobie Matthew's private library of over 3,000 volumes – at that time the largest in England – which effectively re-founded the Minster Library. The chapel also contains the Minster's memorial to Queen Victoria in the form of the very colourful reredos of the

Left Gilded head of a king from the reredos, early 20th century

Nativity. Designed by the architect G. F. Bodley, it was painted and gilded in 1923 and depicts the Holy Family with the shepherds and the wise men. The tomb of Archbishop Richard Scrope (died 1405) separates the Lady Chapel from the adjoining St Stephen's Chapel. Scrope was the first archbishop to be sentenced to death by a lay court, for treason against Henry IV, but many saw him as a martyr and his tomb became a focus of pilgrimage, with a cult growing up for his canonisation that was eventually suppressed. Badly damaged in the 1829 fire, his tomb was restored in 1972 at the expense of the Scrope family. Today, the chapel is regularly used for the daily celebration of Holy Communion, for smaller services of 40–50 people, and is often also the venue for talks such as the Lenten address.

Top left The Chancellor, Glyn Webster, celebrating Holy Communion
Above left Detail from the wall tablet to Ranulph Hurlestone, died 1587
Above Statue of Bishop Skirlaw of Durham, who paid for the Great East window

…alone of all the great Churches in England had best ben preserv'd from the furie of the sacrilegious

Diary of John Evelyn, 1654

Great East Window

Above and right Details from the Great East window and the altar screen
Far right The Great East window

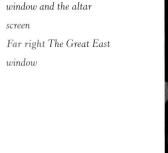

The glory of the east end of the Minster is undoubtedly the Great East window. Made between 1405 and 1408 by John Thornton of Coventry, the foremost master glazier of his day, and his workshop, this is one of the finest medieval windows in the world. Larger than a tennis court, it contains 117 panels in rows of nine, in addition to the tracery. The panels depict the seven days of Creation and events of the Old Testament, followed by a graphic representation of the Book of Revelation. It was intended to make the worshipper mindful of the health of their immortal soul and to show the judgements to come. At the very summit of the window, almost hidden within the tracery, is the figure of God with the words *Ego sum Alpha et Omega* ['I am

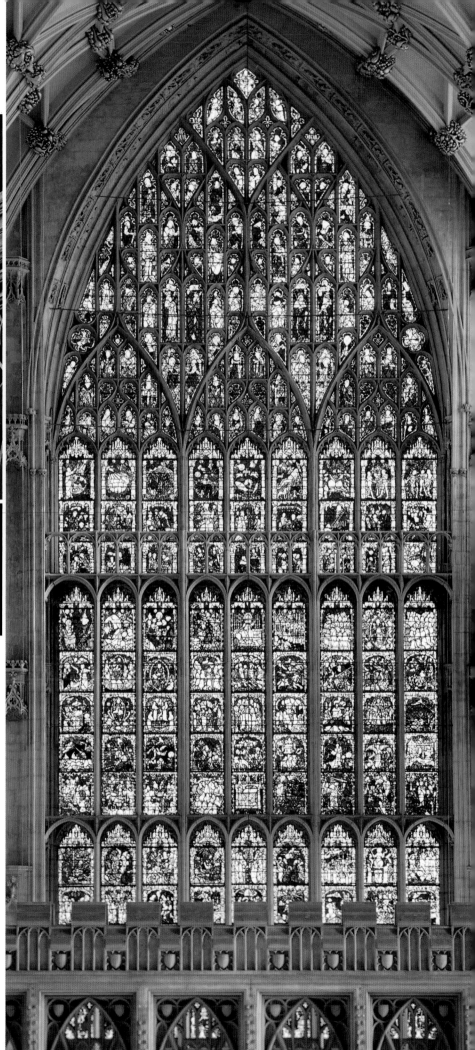

the Beginning and the End']. Contemporary copies of the Dean and Chapter's contract with Thornton survive, which show he was paid £56, the cost being met by Walter Skirlaw, Bishop of Durham, who is depicted in the window. Thornton received a £10 bonus for finishing on time, but according to his contract had risked being paid nothing if the Dean and Chapter didn't like the finished window! The bottom rows contain historical figures and kings, many of them mythical. This masterpiece, together with the entire east end of the Minster, is undergoing a long-term programme of extensive restoration, which will ensure its beauty is secure for the centuries to come.

St Stephen's Chapel

*Above left Detail from
the terracotta reredos
by Tinworth*

*Above Window, mid
14th century, showing
L-R: St Stephen,
St Christopher and
St Lawrence*

*Far right Statue of
Mother Teresa by
Stephenson*

T he northern corner of the east end was re-dedicated as St Stephen's Chapel in 1937, when the beautiful terracotta panel of the *First Hour of the Crucifixion* by George Tinworth (1843–1913) was installed. The panel is set into part of the reredos that had formerly been at the high altar. The altar frontal of Chinese silk from Macao, embroidered all over with flowers, dates from 1720 and was acquired by Dean Milner-White (dean 1941–63) as part of his vision to restore some of the colour and richness of the medieval Minster. The theme of flowers continues in the textiles of this chapel with the delicate embroidery of the kneelers. Worked by the Minster's Broderers' Guild in 1981, to a design by Joan Freeman, they depict 70 of the flowers of the world, ranging from

the Arctic poppy to the flowers of Africa, the Far East and the Americas. The international theme in this chapel is continued with the bust of Mother Teresa of Calcutta, on loan from the sculptor J. Stephenson. Cast in resin-bonded copper, it was made in 1981. The monument, signed 'Fisher sculpt', to Dr John Dealtry (died 1773) on the north wall is unusual in having an epitaph written by the poet William Mason, then Precentor of the Minster. It depicts the Greek goddess Hygeia in mourning for the loss of Dr Dealtry, who was a physician of great renown in his day – reflecting the eighteenth-century fashion for depicting appropriate gods of the ancient world on funerary monuments.

Let languid mortals with beseeching eyes, implore my feeble aid

From the monument to Dr Dealtry, 1773, north wall

The chief beauty of the aisles of the quire is the glass in the windows… amongst the finest glass in the Minster

Minster Guidebook, 1930

North Quire Aisle

Formerly the main route to the shrine of St William, the north quire aisle contains the Minster's only royal tomb, a reconstructed chantry chapel, and the stunning St William window. The tomb of Prince William of Hatfield, son of Edward III, has been in several sites around the Minster, but what remains was returned to what is thought to be its original location in 1979. The figure is that of a young boy, but William actually died as a baby aged about four months in 1337. The canopied niche was repainted with the design of red and gold broom twigs, the badge of the Plantagenets, in the 1980s, and was based on original paint traces found on the stone. To the east of the tomb is the soaring St William

Above left View eastwards showing the Savile monument, 1784, by Fisher
Above centre Detail from monument to Prince William of Hatfield
Above right Detail of tomb to Sir Henry Bellasis, 1624
Left Head detail from the monument to Archbishop Richard Sterne, 1683

window, a recently-conserved masterpiece from the workshop of John Thornton, dating from the early fifteenth century, which depicts the life and miracles of Archbishop William Fitzherbert (died 1154). William was canonised in 1227 and his shrine became the focus for pilgrims, including Edward II who carried a bone of St William in his personal collection of relics. On the south side of the aisle is the tomb of Archbishop Thomas Savage (died 1507), which has a reconstructed chantry chapel above it. There were once about 60 such altars in the medieval Minster, attended by up to 20 chantry priests who sang masses for the souls of the dead, but the altars and the priests were swept away in the Reformation.

Above View upward into the quire transept
Top right Weeping 'putto' from the Vice-Admiral Henry Medley memorial, 1784
Above right St Peter holding the Minster, from the Bowet window, c. 1423
Right Angel from the tomb of Archbishop Savage, 1507

Quire

Above Eagle lectern, 1686
Above right Mouse
'signature' by Kilburn carver
'Mousey' Thompson on the
sanctuary railings
Top The archbishop's throne

As with many cathedrals, York has a quire enclosed by screens, which originally prevented the unprepared and 'unshriven' laity from seeing the Mass. The quire is where services are traditionally sung and where the archbishop has his throne or *cathedra*. Along the sides are the stalls of the canons, each with its badge or plaque showing the prebend to which the canonry belongs. The prebendal estates were originally the source of income that provided the canons with their livelihood. All the original woodwork, the roof, and some of the stonework was lost in the fire of 1829, which was started by the religious fanatic, Jonathan Martin, and completely gutted the quire. However, it was faithfully recreated

...a faire large high Organ, newly built
richly gilt, carv'd & painted &
a sweet snowy Crew of singers

Capt. Hammond, 1634

Above View eastwards of
the quire, restored 1830s
Above right Pinnacles
from the screen
Right Stone painted
shields, including the
'arma Christi', or fictive
heraldry, of Christ, based
on the instruments of the
Passion
Overleaf The quire
looking westwards,
showing the archbishop's
throne to the left and the
pulpit on the right

in the 1830s, thanks to detailed drawings that had been made of all the quire stalls and roof bosses only a few years before the fire. The only major omission was the decision not to recreate the misericords, but instead to put in the fixed seats that are there today. High above on the walls between the arches are the colourful shields and badges of the nobility who originally helped to fund the building of the Minster in the Middle Ages; higher still are the fourteenth-century windows of the quire clerestory with their great figures of saints and kings. It is in the quire that evensong is sung most days, either by the girls' or boys' choir of the Minster, with the Songmen, or by one of the many visiting choirs who ask to sing here.

Right Icon of St Peter, created 2004 as a gift to the incoming Dean from the cathedral of Exeter
Above and above right Central medallion of the high altar cross showing the Virgin Mary and Christ

High Altar

Right Communion preparation with a chalice from the Millennium silver set

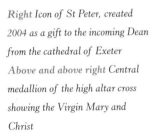

Once this area would have been dominated by the towering shrine of St William, located behind the high altar and accessed through a wooden screen, but now the eye is drawn beyond the screen to the Great East window. The high altar is the *sanctus sanctorum* or 'holy of holies' and is the focal point within the quire with its six silver candlesticks, frontals, and the Spanish silver-gilt cross donated to the Minster in 1950. The colours of the altar cloths, or frontals, are changed according to the season in the Church's year; they vary from richly embroidered white and gold for festivals such as Christmas and Easter to solemn blues and purples for the penitential seasons of Advent and Lent. During Holy Week, the seven days leading up to Easter,

the altar is dressed in unbleached linen, and on Maundy Thursday all the furnishings of cloth, cross and candlesticks are stripped away, leaving the altar and sanctuary bare. The large and richly coloured carpet in front of the altar is one of a number of Persian and Middle Eastern rugs and carpets, collected by Dean Milner-White to adorn the Minster. Unlike the woodwork of the quire, which dates from the 1830s, the stalls in the sanctuary area around the high altar are the work of woodcarver 'Mousey' Thompson from Kilburn in North Yorkshire and were carved in the early 1940s. His signature, a small wooden mouse, is carved on each of his pieces and there are several examples around the Minster.

... the childish recollection of the service has not faded away, but has ever mingled with the most inspiring thoughts of the public worship of God

Harvey Goodwin, Church Congress Report, 1866

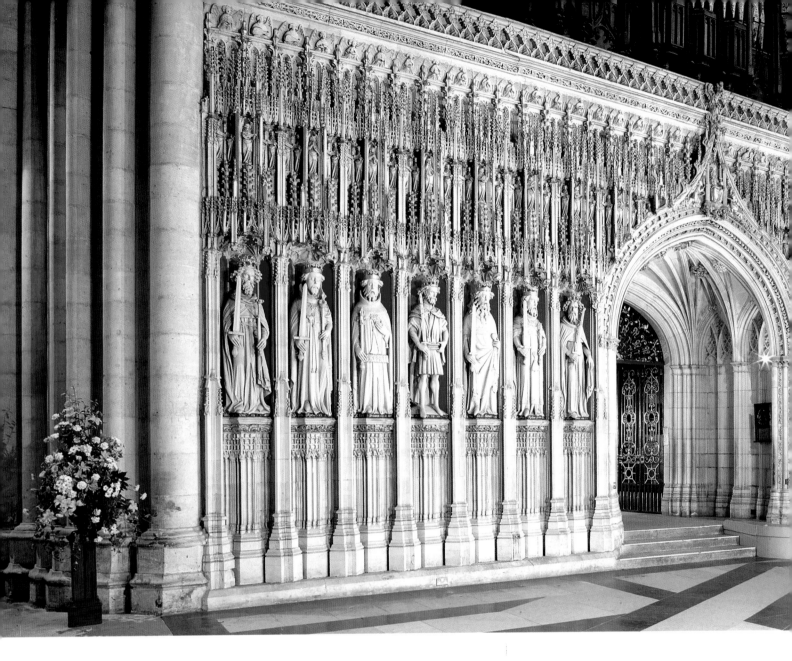

Above View southwards across the screen, showing all fifteen kings
Right The Assumption boss in the roof of the porch to the quire, 15th century

Quire Screen

The design is extraordinary in that the doorway is not central, having seven niches for statues on the north and eight on the south

John H. Harvey, 1977

Also known as the Kings' Screen or the *pulpitum*, the stone screen that forms the western entrance to the quire is one of the most famous parts of the Minster. Carved with 15 near life-size statues of the kings of England, from William the Conqueror to Henry VI, the screen is unusual in being asymmetrical, with the doorway off-centre, seven statues on one side, and eight on the other. The most likely explanation is that the substantial screen was originally designed around 1420 as part of the strengthening of the arches of the eastern end (following the tower collapse of 1407); the intention was to have 14 statues of the kings up to Henry V, but his unexpectedly short reign (1413–1422) necessitated a hasty revision in

Top Detail of the head of King John
Above View upwards into the lantern of the central tower
Above right Angel playing a lute

order to include a statue of Henry VI, who was later murdered. This statue apparently attracted 'improper reverence' and was removed and replaced several times (including once with a statue of James I, now in Ripon Cathedral), before finally being replaced with the present statue by Michael Taylor in 1810. Traces of the original paint that once made these statues brightly coloured can still be detected, and an idea of the effect can be had by looking at the beautiful fifteenth-century Assumption boss of the Virgin in the vaulting of the doorway into the quire. Above the kings is a row of angels playing courtly musical instruments and above that a frieze of more prosaic angels playing instruments such as Northumbrian pipes, serpents and sackbuts!

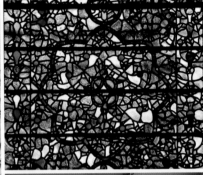

Above left Detail of grisaille glass from the Five Sisters window, c. 1250
Left The astronomical clock, dedicated 1955
Above Copy of a scene in the life of St Nicholas by Crivelli, painted 1930 in memory of Lawrence, 1st Marquess of Zetland
Right Detail of the Hindley clock face

Above The Hindley clock, with sixteenth-century moving figures 'Gog' and 'Magog'
Right Statue of "Our Saviour with Cross" by Fisher, c. 1761, presented to York Minster in 1907

North Transept

The Five Sisters window characterises the austere beauty of the north transept. Built in the mid thirteenth century, largely at the expense of the Sub-dean John Romanus, the transept's architecture is Early English, a style favoured by the Cistercians. The window is filled with grisaille glass – clear glass etched with fine black lines and set into geometric designs with jewel-like points of coloured glass making the pattern. The colourful figurative panel of Habbakuk inserted into the window is much earlier glass, c.1150, from the Norman Minster. On the west side of the transept is St John's Chapel, a regimental chapel for the King's Own Yorkshire Light Infantry, dedicated in 1926. On the east side is the St Nicholas Chapel,

with a colourful altar frontal showing the life of St Nicholas. The Women's Screen, a memorial to the women of the Empire who died serving in World War I, separates this chapel from the astronomical clock, a memorial to the Allied aircrews who flew from airbases in Yorkshire and the North-East and lost their lives in World War II. On one face is shown the precise position of the sun in relation to the Minster at any time, and on the other, the position of the northern stars by which aircrew navigated at night. Dedicated in 1955, the memorial also contains an illuminated Book of Remembrance. Today the transept is often the setting for exhibitions by artists inspired by the Minster and its work, or by groups working to improve people's lives.

The middle chapel, now known as St Nicholas Chapel, is said on very slight authority to have been that of St Thomas of Canterbury

Minster Guidebook, 1930

Right Detail from the altar frontal showing the life of St Nicholas, 1920s

Chapter House

Above View into the
octagonal Chapter
House, showing the
Virgin and Child statue
at the entrance
Left A satirical carving
of a king with a wild
pig on his head

One of the Minster's hidden delights, the Chapter House is accessed from the eastern corner of the north transept, but is concealed from view by its vestibule, itself an architectural jewel. Completed and in use by 1286, the octagonal room is unusual in not having a central column to support the great vaulted roof: instead the weight of the roof is suspended from the exterior dome. Used from the 1290s onwards for parliaments by Edward I and Edward II during their campaigns against the Scots, the Chapter House is still used for meetings of the full College of Canons and for the installation of new canons. Around the walls are the 44 seats of the chapter; each canon has an equal voice in decision-making and the dean is 'first amongst

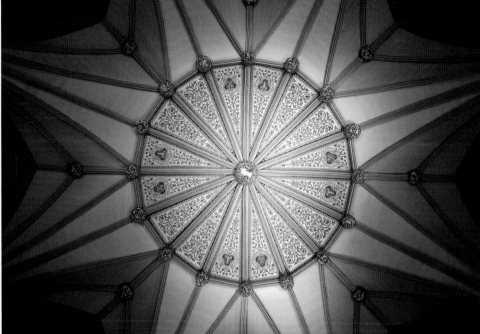

Above Painted ceiling, restored 1845, with 'Agnus Dei' central boss
Left, above right and below Details of carvings from the 13th-century stall arcading: a hound; 'the face-puller'; a green man

equals', so the seats are arranged in groups of six, making it impossible for the dean to sit at the 'head' of a meeting. Some of the Minster's finest carvings are to be found around the canopies of these seats: a riot of funny faces, animals and mythical beasts, around 80 per cent are original carvings from 1270–1280 and the remainder were carved by George Peter White during the 1845 Beckwith restoration. This restoration, which sadly had the walls largely scrubbed clean of their remaining wall paintings, also installed the Minton tile floor with its design based on the tracery of the windows. The surviving original ceiling panels, painted in 1280 and replaced in 1798, are on display in the Undercroft.

As the rose is the flower of flowers, so this is the house of houses

Undated medieval inscription in the doorway of the Chapter House

Right A gossiping woman has her nose pecked by an eagle

The Nave

Top left The nave contains two small chapels where candles can be lit as a prayer
Above left Gilded medieval statue of the Virgin and Child inside the Great West door
Above Detail from the entrance into the quire showing the shield of the crossed swords of St Paul
Right The Dean administering Communion

The main body of the Minster, the nave, is the widest Gothic nave in England and was begun in 1291. On the walls above its arches are the shields of the nobles who accompanied Edward I on his campaigns against the Scots and in the glass of the clerestory windows above are those of their successors who came with Edward II. Also in the clerestory are several panels of Norman glass that survive from the earlier Minsters, 'recycled' to save money in the fourteenth century. Several of the large windows of the nave were glazed at the expense of donors who had themselves incorporated into the design and who possibly also paid for masses at the associated chantry altars which were once dotted all around the nave in the medieval period. Two notable

examples are Richard Tunnock, bellfounder, who is depicted praying to St William in a window otherwise filled with the symbols and depictions of his craft, and the donor 'Vincent', who is shown presenting his gift within a window depicting St Vincent. Protruding from the triforium arcading above is the famous dragon's head. This is almost certainly the remains of an elaborate lifting mechanism for raising, by way of a chain through the dragon's mouth, the 50ft (15.2m) high cover known to have adorned the medieval font, but lost at the Reformation. The present font is a movable one by Charles Gurrey, made of sycamore and bronze, incorporating the symbolism of the fish and the water of life.

The nave roof was completely destroyed by fire in 1840 and the medieval bosses lost.

Above Graeme Wilson's striking tester over St Cuthbert's Chapel dates from 1982 and depicts St Cuthbert's Vision of Heaven with Christ in Glory

Overleaf The nave is usually emptied of chairs in January and part of February to allow people to enjoy the magnificent proportions

… the body of the Church is large and I think larger than any Cathedrall I have seen…: all the isles are broad, the people of fashion use them to walke in…

Diary of Celia Fiennes, 1685

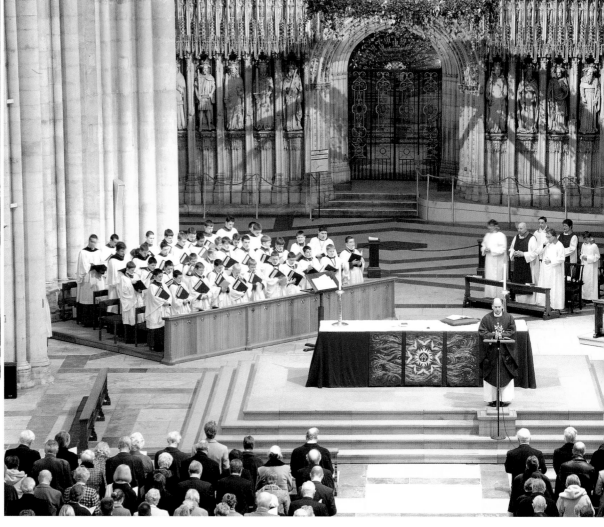

*The dragon's head is
thought to be part of a
medieval mechanism to
raise the now-vanished
font cover*

All of the eight key bosses, each about 3ft (1m) across, which portray the life of Christ and the Blessed Virgin Mary, were replaced with exact replicas – except the Nativity boss: Victorian sensibilities demanded that the Virgin should be depicted bottle-feeding the infant Christ! After the Reformation swept away the altars and shrines of the medieval Minster, the nave was left largely bare. It was filled during the Commonwealth period with York citizens who flocked to hear the preachers and sing psalms, but during the eighteenth and early nineteenth centuries it was primarily a secular space where local gentry could enjoy a stroll in the dry or listen to a concert. The nave had no seating except the stone sills around the walls, until the 1860s, when Dean Duncombe introduced

benches to encourage attendance at services 'by the labouring classes'. Prior to that, all services other than major processions were confined to the quire. Today, the nave, with its nave altar adorned by the cross and candlesticks of the Millennium silver set, is in weekly use for Sunday services and is regularly filled with people attending one of the many services for specific groups and organisations. Able to seat around 2,000 people, it is also a venue for concerts and large events, where the Christian community in the area can use the vastness of the space in a variety of ways.

The Great West window, known as 'the heart of Yorkshire' because of its central tracery, was built 1338–9 by master mason Ivo de Raghtan and was glazed by Master Richard Ketelbarn under the direction of Archbishop Melton. It illustrates the

Right The vaulting and
bosses of the nave were
replaced after the 1840
fire with exact replicas,
except that the Virgin
feeds the infant Christ
with a bottle!

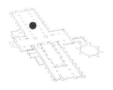

authority and purpose of the Church in the form of a hierarchy going up the window. The bottom row contains eight archbishops of York, including Melton, above which are the Apostles from whom the archbishops derive their authority. Above them are four pairs of panels of the life of Christ and the Virgin, namely the Annunciation, Nativity, Resurrection and Ascension, as preached by the Apostles, and finally, surmounting it all, is a scene set in heaven showing Mary crowned as Queen with Christ at her side. The stonework of the window had to be completely replaced in 1989–90, due to the effects of pollution and erosion, with the exterior arches of the doorway beneath the window being replaced in 1998. These include one row or 'order' which is a new interpretation of the events of the Book of Genesis, to a design

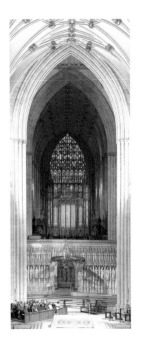

Above The great windows
of the clerestory fill the nave
with light
Above right and below The
very decorative Victorian
pipes on top of the organ are
just some of the 5,300 needed

by Rory Young. Created by the Minster's carvers, the figurative stones are carved beneath canopies where the artistry and imagination of the carvers themselves have been given full reign, following the tradition of centuries. The continuous work of maintenance on the Minster ensures that the traditional skills are not only kept alive, but allowed to flourish, ensuring that the Minster continues to evolve as each age makes its contribution.

The organ above the Kings' Screen was entirely replaced after the 1829 fire and has been restored and worked on many times subsequently, most recently in 1993, so it now has over 5,300 pipes. It is clear from the archives that an organ of some sort has been used in the Minster since at least the fourteenth century, and in the sixteenth century there were several, including at least one 'great organ', probably situated in the quire. The organ has not always been on top of the screen: in 1631 the Dean and Chapter applied to the Crown to use a £1,000 fine they had received towards a new organ and this was installed in 1634, but – at the request of King Charles I – it was placed on the north side of the quire, where it would not obstruct the view of the east window from the nave. This was completely pulled down during the Civil War, so that no trace remained, but following the Restoration in 1660, plans were immediately put into effect to restore an organ to the Minster, and certainly one was in use again by 1666. By 1688 it was back in its original place on the screen, where an organ has remained ever since. Today, the organ is in daily use for services and is frequently used for recitals and concerts by organists from all over the world.

From earliest times…

*Above 13th-century painted
panel fragment from the original
Chapter House ceiling, showing an
archbishop (possibly Walter Gray or
St William)*
*Top right Gilded boss removed from
the north transept ceiling during
repairs in the 1950s*
*Above right Panel of glass, c.1150,
from a Jesse Tree window, showing a
biblical king (possibly David)*
*Right Capital with traces of
original colour from Thomas of
Bayeux's cathedral, c. 1080*

The first known building on the Minster site was not a church at all, but the army headquarters fortress, founded in AD 71, from which the Romans administered the north of England. The remains of this fortress and its four-hundred-year history surround you here in the Undercroft, lying at roughly a 45-degree orientation to the present Minster. It was here, whilst on a visit to York, that Constantine was hailed as Caesar by the troops after his father's death, and Constantine who declared Christianity to be a permitted religion within the empire some six years later, in AD 312. The Saxon wooden Minster, built by King Edwin in 627 for Saint Paulinus, and its stone successors were not found during the archaeological excavations of 1967–73

that were undertaken as part of the huge rescue operation to underpin the Minster and prevent its collapse. What they did uncover, in addition to the Roman fortress, were the foundations and magnificent masonry of the Norman cathedral of Thomas of Bayeux. The remains of his massive geometric columns, already uncovered by John Browne, the Victorian antiquary and archaeologist, in 1830, can be seen in the western crypt and give an idea of the scale and magnificence of this building. Elsewhere in the Undercroft you can see the exterior walls, which were later enclosed by those of the present building, and the finely carved doorjambs and capitals that show the crispness of the carving. Thomas's cathedral was extended by Archbishop Roger de Pont L'Èvêque and you can follow the change in building

Above left The Roman wall plaster was found face down during excavations, which had helped to preserve its vivid colours
Above right Column stumps from the Norman cathedral of Thomas of Bayeux, c. 1080
Left Detail from a 13th-century painted panel fragment from the original Chapter House ceiling, showing the figure of Synagoggia

A lofty city with walls and towers

Alcuin, 8th century

outlines in the floor of the eastern crypt. Set into
the far eastern wall of this crypt is the mysterious
'York Virgin', rediscovered after the 1829 fire set
into the wall of the quire. Deliberately defaced
to be re-used as building stone, the date of her
carving is still being researched, but she could be
as early as tenth-century and therefore be the only
known fragment of the lost Saxon Minster.

The Undercroft exhibition takes you on a
journey through time, from the Roman fortress to
the modern concrete foundations. Many of the
Minster's treasures, both from the archaeological
excavations and other collections, are on display.
These include some of the grave-markers of the
Anglo-Scandinavian inhabitants of the site and
the exquisitely carved 'vine-scroll' fragment of an
unfinished cross-shaft, dating from the eighth

Above View of the tomb
of St William: a re-used
Roman sarcophagus sits
amid a 1970s mosaic of
the River Ouse, backed by
a mosaic of William by
Graeme Wilson

Right Figure of Adam from
the Genesis order replaced
on the Great West door

Far right The York Virgin:
Romanesque, or possibly
earlier, relief of the Virgin
and Child, found in the east
end fabric in 1830

Far left The Treasury,
showing the Genesis stones

century, thought to be one of
the finest examples of carving
of this period in existence. The
Treasury is a display of Minster
silver and treasures, but also
contains a large amount of
parish silver, held on deposit
for safekeeping by the Minster
as part of its support for the
dioceses of the Northern
Province, in its role as Mother Church. In the restored
western crypt now resides the relocated body of
St William, at rest after his many moves. A central
symbol of the life of the medieval Minster, he now lies
in a modern setting but in a Roman sarcophagus, thus
enshrining the three major phases of the Minster's life
and uniting our history with the present day.

Visitors checklist

The exterior shop,
York Minster Gifts, in
Minster Gates

Opening Times

Daily for early services from 7.00am
For sightseeing:
Mon–Sat: 9.00am (9.30am November–March)
– last entry 4.45pm
Sunday: 12.00 noon–3.45pm
Opening times may change subject to major cathedral services; please check in advance of your visit to avoid disappointment.

Service Times

Mon–Sat: 7.30am; 7.45am; 12.30pm; 5.00pm
Sunday: 8.00am; 10.00am; 11.30am; 4.00pm

Admission

Entry charges apply for the Minster, the Undercroft and the Tower.

Guided tours are offered free of charge by our team of voluntary guides (when available).

Shop

The Minster has two main shops, one located off the nave and the other just outside the Minster in Minster Gates. They sell a wide range of souvenir and gift items, many based on, or inspired by, the Minster and its collections. You can also visit our on-line shop via the Minster's website.

Group Bookings

Can be arranged – please contact the Visitors' Department – tel: 01904 557216 or email: visitors@yorkminster.org

School Visits

Can be arranged through the Centre for School Visits – tel: 01904 557224 or email: csv@yorkminster.org

Conferences and Events

Can be arranged by contacting St William's College – tel: 01904 557233 or email: conference@yorkminster.org

Disabled Access

Ground Level and Precincts
A permanent stone ramp has been constructed at the west end of the Minster. A temporary ramp is in place outside the south door. Inside, there is a ramp from the nave into the quire and from the north transept to the Chapter House.

A welcome and information leaflet is available for visitors with disabilities.

Assistance dogs are welcomed at the Minster. Wheelchairs for use in the Minster are available on request. Toilet facilities are available for use by disabled visitors.

Disabled parking facilities are available by prior arrangement.

Further Information

For more information on these topics please contact York Minster Visitors' Department – tel: 01904 557216 or email: visitors@yorkminster.org, or York Minster Police – tel: 01904 557222.

Contact details

York Minster, Deangate, York, YO1 7HH
or contact the Visitors Department –
tel: 01904 557216 or
email: visitors@yorkminster.org
website: www.yorkminster.org

First published in 2005 by Jarrold Publishing, Whitefriars, Norwich NR3 1JR
Telephone 01603 677318   www.jarrold-publishing.co.uk

Text by Louise Hampson, Collections Manager, York Minster. Photographs by Peter Smith of Newbery Smith Photography, except:
Martin Sheppard, p.1 (the Dean); Jim Kershaw, p.3 (library across park) and p.19 (Great East window – whole window);
Tom French, pp.18,19 (details of Great East window).
ISBN 0-7117-4156-5
Designed and produced by Jarrold Publishing. Printed in Great Britain 1/05